Bible Word Comparison

Four Traditional Bibles Compared with Twelve Contemporary Bibles

Third Millennium Publications

Compiled and edited by William D. Prindle, J. D. Ret.

Bible Word Comparison
Copyright © 1998 by Deuel Enterprises, Inc.
Gary, SD 57237
Library of Congress Catalog Card Number 98-61723
ISBN 1-892833-01-8
Published by Third Millennium Publications®
A division of Deuel Enterprises, Inc.
1111 North Coteau Street
Gary, SD 57237 USA

Table of Contents

Introduction

A phenomenon of the last third of the twentieth century has been the astonishing proliferation of contemporary Bible translations, all containing differing messages. Sociologists and theologians may disagree as to the cause of this phenomenon, but the stark fact is that the sacred Word of God, which has been both divinely inspired and providentially preserved from the earliest times to the present day, has been altered in innumerable ways by contemporary translators involving changes in language, meaning, and theology.

It must be remembered that what modern translators are attempting to change is not the wording of a transitory document, but the holy and blessed Word of God. Can we through our silence suffer this to happen? Is not the Word of God eternal? Does not also the twentieth century have a responsibility to transmit the unsullied Word to generations to come?

The nature and magnitude of this gross and tragic contemporary development is the subject of this *Bible Word Comparison*.

It is the position of the compiler of this study that the large number of translations of the Scriptures is evidence of an underlying translator hostility toward many of the great ideas and thoughts that have characterized over 3,000 years of Jewish-Christian cultural history. We point out specifically that many modern translators and their client Bible publishers too often reflect the negative aspects of the post-Enlightenment era. We assert that the social and cultural orientation of many modern translators has influenced negatively their translating efforts. Modern translators of the holy Word of God have actually politicized, in multifaceted manifestations, their Bible translating efforts. Not only have they demeaned and downgraded the exalted diction of traditional Biblical English, but they have also contaminated biblical idiom with political ideas and concepts alien to the spirit and tenor of the Scriptures. Twentieth-century materialism and secularism, and also the influence of special interest groups, have each impacted to one degree or another most modern Bible translations, as has the Gnosticism of an ancient Egyptian and Hellenistic heretical culture.

In our approach to the problems posed by modern Bible translations, we broaden the scope of previous comparative word studies. Earlier word studies have compared wording in the *Authorized (King James) Version* with a few contemporary versions. In this *Bible Word Comparison*, we compare selected texts of four

Traditional Bibles with twelve widely used Contemporary Bibles. The Traditional Bibles used in this comparison are the following:

1.) The *Authorized Version* of 1611, commonly known as the *King James Version*, which served as the dominant Protestant Bible for approximately 375 years;

2.) The *Douay-Rheims Version*, the Catholic version of 1609, which served as the principal Catholic English translation for over 350 years;

3.) The *21st Century King James Version* (1994), an updating of the 66 books commonly found in the Old and New Testaments of the *King James Version*;

4.) The *Third Millennium Bible* (1998), an updating of all 80 books of the original *Authorized (King James) Version* of A.D. 1611.

To compare with the four Traditional Bibles enumerated above we have selected the following frequently used Contemporary Bibles:

1.) *Contemporary English Version* (1995)
2.) *God's Word* (1995)
3.) *New American Bible* (1970)
4.) *New American Standard Bible, Updated* (1997)
5.) *New International Version* (1973)
6.) *New Jerusalem Bible* (1985)
7.) *New King James Version* (1982)
8.) *New Living Translation* (1996)
9.) *New Revised Standard Version* (1989)
10.) *The New Testament and Psalms: An Inclusive Version* (*Oxford University Press*, 1995)
11.) *Revised English Bible* (1989)
12.) *Today's English Version* (1976)

Before discussing specific word comparisons, we list in the following paragraphs five major differences between Traditional Bibles and Contemporary Bibles:

1.) Traditional Bible translators use a more *formal, literal,* and *precise* translating technique than is used in Contemporary Bibles. Most Contemporary Bibles reflect a less precise technique, known as *dynamic equivalence.* In essence, this latter technique results in translations which, in the mere subjective opinions of the translators, purport to reflect the *meanings* rather than the text, and are allegedly more in accord with the presumed intentions of the original writers. Some contemporary translators use an even more extreme translating technique referred to as *paraphrase;* wherein the translator simply decides approximately what the original writers may have meant, and then casts it in modern colloquial English. The use of these nonliteral translating techniques accounts for much of the flood of differing readings found in Contemporary Bibles.

2.) Traditional Bibles all employ *Biblical English.* Contemporary Bibles use the secular, colloquial English currently in use in commerce and the media. *Biblical English* has been the historic language of liturgy, worship, and prayer. It is not, as has often been alleged, *Elizabethan* or *Shakespearean* language. *Biblical English*, in fact, has never at any time been the popular or spoken language anywhere. It is the language reserved exclusively for the holy Scriptures and for liturgy, worship, and prayer. It owes its character to the faithful and literal translation from the original biblical languages into English. It has as a matter of history found its acceptance in Scriptures for more than five hundred years in over ninety percent of the English-speaking churches throughout the world. Only in the last half of the twentieth century does one find secular, colloquial English being used in Bible translations.

3.) The New Testament Greek text of Traditional Bibles, used continuously for almost two thousand years, is generally referred to as the *Ecclesiastical Text* or the *Byzantine-Antiochian Text.* The text used as a basis for Contemporary Bibles is dramatically different, and is referred to among scholars as the *Alexandrian* cluster of texts. This text was unused and ignored in the Christian community for over fifteen hundred years, and was first used in an English-language Bible translation in 1881. Since then it has become the basis for most Contemporary Bibles. The *Alexandrian Text* used in Contemporary Bibles contains almost 3,000 fewer words than the traditional text, and reflects the secular bias of the ancient Hellenistic and Alexandrian culture of the third century A.D.

4.) Most modern Protestant Bibles omit books, totaling over 126,000 words, contained in the *Authorized (King James) Version* of 1611. These omitted books are known as the Apocrypha/ Deuterocanonical Books. The Apocrypha/Deuterocanonical Books in the *Authorized Version* of 1611 are: 1st and 2nd Esdras, Tobit, Judith, The Rest of the Chapters of the Book of Esther, The Wisdom of Solomon, Ecclesiasticus, Baruch, The Song of the Three Holy Children, Susanna, Bel and the Dragon, The Prayer of Manasseh, and 1st and 2nd Maccabees. All but two of these books are found in the *Douay-Rheims Version.* Most of these books were included in the original editions of the most widely used Bibles of the last six hundred years, including the *Wycliffe Bible* (1382), the *Coverdale Bible* (1535), the *Great Bible* (1539), the *Geneva Bible* (1560), the *Bishop's Bible* (1568), the *Douay-Rheims Version* (1609), and the *Authorized Version* (1611). These beautiful writings were also included in the original German *Luther Bible*, the Latin

Vulgate, the Syriac *Peshitta*, and Ethiopic Ge`ez, Armenian, Coptic, and Old Church Slavonic versions. In addition, these books were included in the *Septuagint*, the Greek Old Testament used by the Apostolic Church. For reasons never widely publicized, and without adequate advance public knowledge or discussion, these books were removed from the *Authorized Version* by agreement among the publishers and certain special interest groups approximately two hundred years after the original printing, and have not yet reappeared in most Protestant Bibles.

5.) The actual wording of the Scriptures has been changed in Contemporary Bibles in hundreds of instances. Plainly stated, many Contemporary Bibles have adapted God's Word to accommodate to recent secular social and political trends through the use of gender-neutral language and other forms of socio-linguistic engineering, currently referred to as "political correctness." This development in modern translations is truly a lamentable attempt to modify the Word of God to conform to the prevailing secular culture.

In the balance of this *Bible Word Comparison* we will be discussing specific examples (among many) of theological, linguistic, social, and political biases which have been incorporated into modern translations. We suggest that the reader focus attention primarily on the specific biblical words being compared rather than on the comments of the compiler. Though necessarily subjective, our remarks are based on forty years of legal experience in studying and evaluating the meaning and nuances of English words, together with years of comparative study of English-language Bibles. But, if you do not agree with our comments, ask yourself how best to explain the enormous differences in both text and meaning between Contemporary Bibles and Traditional Bibles. Work out your own explanation as to how and why these substantial differences developed in translations of the inspired Word of God.

Abbreviations Used in Comparisons
Traditional Bibles

(Listed in alphabetical order of their abbreviations)

Abbreviations	Titles	First Published
AV	*Authorized Version* *(King James Version)*	1611
D-R	*Douay-Rheims Version* (Original Catholic English Version) Tan Books and Publishers	1609
KJ21	*21st Century King James Version* KJ21 Bible Publishers	1994
TMB	*Third Millennium Bible* Third Millennium Publications	1998

[The *21st Century King James Version* and the *Third Millennium Bible* are not new translations but careful *updatings* of the *Authorized (King James) Version* of 1611.]

Abbreviations Used in Comparisons
Contemporary Bibles

(Listed in alphabetical order of their abbreviations)

Abbreviations	Titles	First Published
CEV	*Contemporary English Version* Thomas Nelson Publishers	1995
GW	*God's Word* World Publishing	1995
NAB	*New American Bible* Catholic Book Publishing Co.	1970
NASBU	*New American Standard Bible Updated* Lockman Foundation Foundation Publications, Inc.	1995
NIV	*New International Version* International Bible Society Zondervan Publishing House	1973
NJB	*New Jerusalem Bible* Doubleday and Company, Inc.	1985
NKJ	*New King James Version* Thomas Nelson Publishers	1982
NLT	*New Living Translation* Tyndale House Publishers, Inc.	1996
NRSV	*New Revised Standard Version* Thomas Nelson Publishers	1989
OxI	*New Testament And Psalms —* *An Inclusive Version* Oxford University Press	1995
REB	*Revised English Bible* *with the Apocrypha* Oxford University Press Cambridge University Press	1989
TEV	*Today's English Version* *(Good News Bible)* American Bible Society	1976

Bible Word Comparison
Old Testament

Genesis 1:28

AV	Be **fruitful,** and multiply, and **replenish the earth**, and subdue it ...
D-R	**Increase** and multiply, and **fill the earth**, and subdue it...
KJ21	"Be **fruitful** and multiply, and **replenish the earth,** and subdue it...
TMB	"Be **fruitful** and multiply, and **replenish the earth,** and subdue it...

CEV	**Have a lot of children! Fill the earth** with people and bring it under your control.
GW	"Be **fertile**, increase in number, **fill the earth**...
NAB	"Be **fertile** and multiply; **fill the earth** and subdue it.
NASBU	"Be **fruitful** and multiply, and **fill the earth**, and subdue it...
NIV	"Be **fruitful** and increase in number; **fill the earth** and subdue it.
NJB	'Be **fruitful**, multiply, **fill the earth** and subdue it...
NKJ	"Be **fruitful** and multiply; **fill the earth** and subdue it...
NLT	"**Multiply** and **fill the earth** and subdue it.
NRSV	"Be **fruitful** and multiply, and **fill the earth** and subdue it...
REB	'Be **fruitful** and increase, **fill the earth** and subdue it...
TEV	"**Have many children**, so that **your descendants will live all over the earth** and bring it under their control.

Comment

Three Traditional Bibles speak of the duty of mankind to **replenish** the earth's exhaustible resources. Herein is found the biblical answer to such environmental questions as population growth, pollution, and the restoration of the earth's natural resources which are currently being consumed at a prodigal rate. The admonition by God to replenish the earth imposes a duty on every human being to be frugal, to waste nothing, and to be acutely concerned about environmental and conservation issues.

Genesis 2:7

AV	...and man became a **living soul**.
D-R	...and man became a **living soul**.
KJ21	...and man became a **living soul**.
TMB	...and man became a **living soul**.

CEV	...and the man **started breathing**.
GW	The man became a **living being**.
NAB	...and so man became a **living being**.
NASBU	...and man became a **living being**.
NIV	...and man became a **living being**.
NJB	...and man became a **living being**.
NKJ	...and man became a **living being**.
NLT	And the man became a **living person**.
NRSV	...and the man became a **living being**.
REB	...he became a **living creature**.
TEV	...and the man **began to live**.

Comment

The biblical characterization of man as having a **soul**, clearly set forth in the Traditional Bibles, is being challenged in Contemporary Bibles, with consequent blurring of the fundamental difference in kind between human beings and all other forms of life. Modern secular scientific circles challenge the existence of a soul, affirming as reality only what can be observed, measured, and demonstrated scientifically. Most Contemporary Bibles reflect the increasing influence of a modern-day type of Gnosticism in the garb of secular humanism. Note that in the NIV alone the word **soul** has been replaced by another word in 397 places.

Genesis 17:1

AV	Walk before me, and be thou **perfect**.
D-R	...walk before me, and be **perfect**.
KJ21	Walk before Me, and be thou **perfect**.
TMB	Walk before Me, and be thou **perfect**.

CEV	If you obey me and **always do right,**
GW	Live in my presence **with integrity**.
NAB	Walk in my presence and be **blameless**.
NASBU	Walk before Me, and be **blameless**.
NIV	...walk before me and be **blameless**.
NJB	Live in my presence, be **perfect**...
NKJ	...walk before Me and be **blameless**.
NLT	...serve me faithfully and live a **blameless** life.
NRSV	...walk before me, and be **blameless**.
REB	Live always in my presence and be **blameless**...
TEV	Obey me and always do **what is right**.

Comment

God mandates that man strive toward nothing short of perfection. This is properly emphasized in Traditional Bibles. Compare this mandate with the wording of Contemporary Bibles, where lesser levels of achievement are mentioned and condoned. **Blameless** is a lesser standard and falls far short of perfection.

Exodus 7:13

AV   And **he hardened** Pharaoh's heart...
D-R   And Pharao's heart was **hardened**...
KJ21 And **He hardened** Pharaoh's heart...
TMB   And **He hardened** Pharaoh's heart...

CEV   The King behaved just as the LORD had said and **stubbornly refused** to listen.
GW   Yet, Pharaoh continued to be **stubborn**...
NAB   Pharaoh, however, was **obstinate**...
NASBU Yet Pharaoh's heart **was hardened**...
NIV   Yet Pharaoh's heart **became hard**...
NJB   Pharaoh, however, **remained obstinate**...
NKJ   And Pharaoh's heart **grew hard**...
NLT   Pharaoh's heart, however, remained **hard and stubborn**.
NRSV Still Pharaoh's **heart was hardened**...
REB   Pharaoh, however, **was obstinate**...
TEV   The king, however, **remained stubborn**...

Comment

Question: Did God harden Pharaoh's heart, or was Pharaoh's stubbornness and cruelty a result of his own will, as implied in most Contemporary Bibles? Exodus 9:16 and Romans 9:17-18 provide the answer to this question.

4

Exodus 20:13

AV	Thou shalt not **kill**.
D-R	Thou shalt not **kill**.
KJ21	Thou shalt not **kill**.
TMB	Thou shalt not **kill**.

CEV	Do not **murder**.
GW	Never **murder**.
NAB	You shall not **kill**.
NASBU	You shall not **murder**.
NIV	You shall not **murder**.
NJB	You shall not **kill**.
NKJ	You shall not **murder**.
NLT	Do not **murder**.
NRSV	You shall not **murder**.
REB	Do not commit **murder**.
TEV	Do not commit **murder**.

Comment

Does God say that human beings shall not kill each other (Traditional Bibles) or, alternatively, that they shall not deprive another person of life in a manner which secular laws and judicial decisions define as murder (Contemporary Bibles)? Note that most modern translators, in using the word **murder** rather than **kill**, have in fact exempted certain types of killing of human beings from the commandment. Examples, among others, are doctor assisted suicide, negligent killing, and euthanasia, none of which are legally considered to be murder. God's Word is that **thou shalt not kill** a human being, not merely that **you shall not murder** a human being.

Exodus 32:25

AV   And when Moses saw that the people were **naked**...
D-R   And when Moses saw that the people were **naked**...
KJ21   And when Moses saw that the people were **naked**...
TMB   And when Moses saw that the people were **naked**...

CEV   And now they had **made fools of themselves** in front of their enemies.
GW   and they became an **object of ridicule** to their enemies.
NAB   Aaron had let the people **run wild**...
NASBU Now when Moses saw that the people were **out of control**...
NIV   Moses saw that the people were **running wild**...
NJB   When Moses saw that the people were **out of hand**...
NKJ   Now when Moses saw that the people were **unrestrained**...
NLT   When Moses saw that Aaron had let the people get **completely out of control**...
NRSV   When Moses saw that the people were **running wild**...
REB   Moses saw that the people were **out of control**...
TEV   Moses saw that Aaron had let the people get **out of control**...

Comment

When Moses returned to the children of Israel from his confrontation with God on Mount Sinai, what did he find happening? Were they **out of control**, or were they **running wild**, or were they the **object of ridicule** to their enemies, etc., or were they **naked**? Note how Traditional Bibles pinpoint specifically the nature of the misconduct: the sinning people were naked. In consequence of this deplorable circumstance, the people had in fact become objects of ridicule; they were in fact running wild; they had gotten out of hand; they were unrestrained; they were completely out of control—all of which were ancillary to, and caused by, their shameless nakedness. Little wonder that our civilization has become debauched in putting such a high premium on nakedness and semi-nakedness.

1 Samuel 8:5

AV	Now make us a king to **judge us**...
D-R	...make us a king, to **judge us**...
KJ21	Now make us a king to **judge us**...
TMB	Now make us a king to **judge us**...

CEV	Now we want a king to **be our leader**...
GW	Now appoint a king to **judge us**...
NAB	...appoint a king over us, as other nations have, to **judge us**.
NASBU	Now appoint a king for us to **judge us**...
NIV	...now appoint a king to **lead us**...
NJB	So give us a king to **judge us**...
NKJ	Now make for us a king to **judge us**...
NLT	Give us a king **like all the other nations have**.
NRSV	...appoint for us, then, a king **to govern us**...
REB	...appoint us a king to **rule us**...
TEV	So then, appoint a king to **rule over us**...

Comment

The traditional renderings reflect a profoundly different concept from that of some Contemporary Bibles in respect to the purpose of government. Is the government for the purpose of judging between good and evil deeds of individual persons, or for the purpose of ruling, governing, and taxing the people to achieve some communal social good as perceived by the governing authorities? There is a difference between the traditional idea of government for the purpose of judging the people according to the standards of God's holy commandments (Traditional Bibles), and the idea of ruling the people by force and coercion to direct their lives into paths which political leaders think best for them (Contemporary Bibles). The biblical view is that of a government which protects people against the unrighteous acts of others, e.g., fraud and violence.

7

Job 42:10

AV	And the Lord **turned the captivity of Job**, when he prayed for his friends...
D-R	The Lord also was **turned at the penance of Job**, when he prayed for his friends.
KJ21	And the Lord **released Job from captivity** when he prayed for his friends.
TMB	And the Lord **released Job from captivity** when he prayed for his friends.

CEV	After Job had prayed for his three friends, the Lord **made Job twice as rich as he had been before**.
GW	After Job prayed for his friends, the LORD **restored Job's prosperity**...
NAB	Also, the LORD **restored the prosperity of Job**...
NASBU	The Lord **restored the fortunes of Job** when he prayed for his friends...
NIV	After Job had prayed for his friends, the Lord **made him prosperous** again...
NJB	And Yahweh **restored Job's condition**, while Job was interceding for his friends.
NKJ	And the Lord **restored Job's losses** when he prayed for his friends.
NLT	When Job prayed for his friends, the Lord **restored his fortunes.**
NRSV	And the Lord **restored the fortunes** of Job when he had prayed for his friends...
REB	...when he had interceded for his friends. The Lord **restored Job's fortunes**...
TEV	Then, after Job had prayed for his three friends, the Lord **made him prosperous** again...

Comment

Traditional Bibles focus on God's releasing Job from the captivity of Satan after Job had participated in the blessed act of intercessory prayer for his friends. Contemporary Bibles, on the other hand, focus on God's rewarding Job for his faithfulness by restoring his material prosperity. In the former, the spiritual aspect of Job's restoration is emphasized; in the latter, his material gain is emphasized.

8

Psalm 84:11

AV	... the Lord will give **grace and glory**...
D-R	(Ps 83:12) ...the Lord will give **grace and glory**.
KJ21	... the Lord will give **grace and glory**...
TMB	... the Lord will give **grace and glory**...

CEV	You treat us with **kindness and with honor**...
GW	The Lord grants **favor and honor**.
NAB	(vs 12)...bestowing all **grace and glory**.
NASBU	The Lord gives **grace and glory**...
NIV	...the Lord bestows **favor and honor**...
NJB	...he gives **grace and glory**...
NKJ	...the Lord will give **grace and glory**...
NLT	He gives us **grace and glory**.
NRSV	...he bestows **favor and honor**.
OxI	...who bestows **favor and honor**.
REB	...**grace and honor** are his to bestow.
TEV	...blessing us with **kindness and honor**.

Comment

Traditional Bibles speak of the Lord's inexpressibly wonderful and blessed gifts of grace and glory. Some Contemporary Bibles refer to matters of lesser magnitude (albeit still of importance), namely, kindness, honor, favor, etc. Here, as in many other passages, Contemporary Bibles lose depth of passion and poetic power when they address less exalted subjects than Traditional Bibles.

Psalm 101:1

AV   I will sing of **mercy and judgment**...
D-R   (Ps 100:1) **Mercy and judgment** I will sing to thee...
KJ21   I will sing of **mercy and judgment**...
TMB   I will sing of **mercy and judgment**...

CEV   I will celebrate your **kindness and your justice.**
GW   I will sing about **mercy and justice.**
NAB   I sing of **love and justice**...
NASBU   I will sing of **lovingkindness** and **justice**...
NIV   I will sing of your **love and justice**...
NJB   I will sing of faithful **love and judgment**...
NKJ   I will sing of **mercy and justice**...
NLT   I will sing of your **love and justice.**
NRSV   I will sing of **loyalty and of justice**...
OxI   I will sing of **loyalty and of justice**...
REB   I shall sing of **loyalty and justice**...
TEV   My song is about **loyalty and justice**...

Comment
The Traditional Bibles allude to two wondrous and mighty biblical blessings, namely, God's judgment against sin and His saving acts of mercy. God's balancing of mercy and judgment is a point entirely lost in this and in similar passages in contemporary translations.

Psalm 111:7

AV	...all his **commandments** are sure.
D-R	(Ps 110:8)All his **commandments** are faithful...
KJ21	...all His **commandments** are sure.
TMB	...all His **commandments** are sure.

CEV	...and his **laws** can be trusted.
GW	All his **guiding principles** are trustworthy.
NAB	...reliable all your **decrees**...
NASBU	All His **precepts** are sure.
NIV	...all his **precepts** are trustworthy.
NJB	...all his **precepts** are trustworthy...
NKJ	...All His **precepts** are sure.
NLT	...and all his **commandments** are trustworthy.
NRSV	...all his **precepts** are trustworthy.
OxI	...all God's **precepts** are trustworthy.
REB	...all his **precepts** are trustworthy...
TEV	...all his **commands** are dependable.

Comment

Traditional Bibles use the word **commandments**, a more intense, powerful and personal word than **precepts, guiding principles** or **laws**. Contemporary Bibles substitute language which is as equally applicable to civil government as it is to the commandments of God. Contemporary language tends to blur the difference between the mandates of the omniscient and omnipotent personal God and the dictates of earthly powers.

Proverbs 11:16

AV   ...and **strong men retain riches.**
D-R   ...and **the strong shall have riches.**
KJ21   ...and **strong men retain riches.**
TMB   ...and **strong men retain riches.**

CEV   ...but a **man must work hard to get rich.**
GW   ...but **ruthless men gain riches.**
NAB   ...but the **diligent gain wealth.**
NASBU ...And **ruthless men attain riches.**
NIV   ...but **ruthless men gain only wealth.**
NJB   ...**violent people acquire wealth.**
NKJ   ...But **ruthless men retain riches.**
NLT   ...and **violent men get rich.**
NRSV   ...but **the aggressive gain riches.**
REB   ...a **bold man gets only a fortune.**
TEV   ...but an **aggressive man will get rich.**

Comment

The inference in Contemporary Bibles is that only ruthless, violent, and aggressive people become wealthy. Contrast this with the lack of prejudice against the possession and accumulation of wealth as such, reflected in the traditional biblical view, a view which correctly reflects 3,000 years of unbroken Jewish-Christian perspective. Strong and powerful men are not necessarily evil because they are rich, nor are the poor necessarily virtuous because they are poor. God looks at the heart.

Proverbs 27:4

AV	...but who is able to stand before **envy**?
D-R	...and who can bear the violence of one provoked?
KJ21	...but who is able to stand before **envy**?
TMB	...but who is able to stand before **envy**?

CEV	...but a **jealous** person is even worse.
GW	...but who can survive **jealousy**?
NAB	...but before **jealousy** who can stand?
NASBU	...But who can stand before **jealousy**?
NIV	...but who can stand before **jealousy**?
NJB	...but **jealousy**, who can withstand that ?
NKJ	...But who is able to stand before **jealousy**?
NLT	...but who can survive the destructiveness of **jealousy**?
NRSV	...but who is able to stand before **jealousy**?
REB	...but who can stand up to **jealousy**?
TEV	...but it is nothing compared to **jealousy**.

Comment

Envy is a word which has fallen out of favor because it describes a deadly sin, a subject which is anathema to the no-fault society in which we live. **Envy** conveys the idea of coveting another's advantages, wealth, or attributes. **Envy** by definition is resentful awareness of the advantages enjoyed by others, together with a powerful desire to possess the property and wealth of others.

Jealousy is the preferred contemporary politically sanitized word, reflecting as it does one person's feeling of inferiority to another and the fear of loss of one's own self esteem. **Jealousy** does not reflect a covetousness of what belongs to another, as does **envy**.

Envy conveys a desire to take what belongs to another. **Jealousy** reflects a fear of losing to another what belongs to one's self.

Proverbs 28:17

AV	A man that doeth violence to the blood of any person **shall flee to the pit...**
D-R	A man that doth violence to the blood of a person, if he **flee even to the pit...**
KJ21	**...shall flee to the pit...**
TMB	**...shall flee to the pit...**

CEV	Make them **stay on the run for as long as they live.**
GW	**...will be a fugitive down to his grave.**
NAB	**...flee to the grave...**
NASBU	A man who is laden with the guilt of human blood **will be a fugitive until death...**
NIV	A man tormented by the guilt of murder **will be a fugitive till death...**
NJB	A man guilty of murder **will flee till he reaches his tomb...**
NKJ	A man burdened with bloodshed **will flee into a pit...**
NLT	A murderer's tormented conscience will **drive him into the grave.**
NRSV	If someone is burdened with the blood of another, **let that killer be a fugitive until death...**
REB	Anyone charged with bloodshed **will jump into a well to escape arrest.**
TEV	A man guilty of murder is **digging his own grave as fast as he can.**

Comment

A glaring weakness among modern translating committees is the wide disagreement as to the *meaning* of the wording in the original language. Notice that the more ancient and literal translations tend to agree in substance because they are more concerned with what the text *says*, while more recent translations vary markedly each from the other because they are trying to decide what the text *means*. This emphasis among modern translators on what they believe the Word of God *means*, rather than on what the text *says*, has caused an unending proliferation of versions, resulting in great confusion among the Bible-reading public.

Proverbs 29:7

AV	The righteous considereth the **cause** of the poor...
D-R	The just taketh notice of the **cause** of the poor...
KJ21	The righteous considereth the **cause** of the poor...
TMB	The righteous considereth the **cause** of the poor...

CEV	The wicked don't care about the **rights** of the poor...
GW	A righteous person knows the just **cause** of the poor.
NAB	The just man has a care for the **rights** of the poor...
NASBU	The righteous is concerned for the **rights** of the poor...
NIV	The righteous care about **justice** for the poor...
NJB	The upright understands the **cause** of the weak...
NKJ	The righteous considers the **cause** of the poor...
NLT	The godly know the **rights** of the poor...
NRSV	The righteous know the **rights** of the poor...
REB	The righteous are concerned for the **claims** of the helpless...
TEV	A good person knows the **rights** of the poor...

Comment

In Traditional Bibles the **cause** of the poor is regarded with great concern and compassion. But Contemporary Bibles focus on the **rights** of the poor, quite a different matter.

In traditional translations the circumstances of the poor are intended to elicit loving compassion by those more fortunate. But in some Contemporary Bibles what should elicit compassion becomes a vehicle for the promotion of the political **rights**, entitlements, and claims on society by the poor. Thus so-called *social justice* supplants compassion for our less fortunate brethren. When godly love for the poor is replaced by legal claims or rights to be politically asserted by the poor, love and compassion vanish and are replaced by class tensions and conflict.

Ecclesiastes 1:2

AV	**Vanity of vanities...**
D-R	**Vanity of vanities...**
KJ21	**"Vanity of vanities...**
TMB	**"Vanity of vanities...**

CEV	**Nothing makes sense!**
GW	**"Absolutely pointless!"**
NAB	**Vanity of vanities...**
NASBU	**"Vanity of vanities...**
NIV	**"Meaningless! Meaningless!"**
NJB	**Sheer futility...**
NKJ	**"Vanity of vanities...**
NLT	**"Everything is meaningless...**
NRSV	**Vanity of vanities...**
REB	**Futility, utter futility...**
TEV	**It is useless, useless...**

Comment

In this highly emotional and poetic passage, which of the translations reflect the inherent beauty, power, and passion of the true Word? The depoeticizing of biblical language and the substitution of banal, uninspiring words occurs with alarming frequency in Contemporary Bibles. When translators deprive biblical language of its beauty, poetry and rhythm, they deprive it likewise of its power. Modern translators rob the Bible of its traditional beauty; little wonder that they are thereby depriving it of its capacity to move men's souls and inspire men to action. One of the greatest mistakes of contemporary translators is the substitution of colloquial secular language for reverent Biblical English.

Ecclesiastes 9:9

AV	**Live joyfully** with the **wife** whom thou lovest...
D-R	**Live joyfully** with the **wife** whom thou lovest...
KJ21	**Live joyfully** with the **wife** whom thou lovest...
TMB	**Live joyfully** with the **wife** whom thou lovest...

CEV	**Life is short**, and you love your **wife**...
GW	**Enjoy life** with your **wife**, whom you love...
NAB	**Enjoy life** with the **wife** whom you love...
NASBU	**Enjoy life** with the **woman** whom you love...
NIV	**Enjoy life** with your **wife**, whom you love...
NJB	**Spend your life** with the **woman** you love...
NKJ	**Live joyfully** with the **wife** whom you love...
NLT	**Live happily** with the **woman** you love...
NRSV	**Enjoy life** with the **wife** whom you love...
REB	**Enjoy life** with a **woman** you love...
TEV	**Enjoy life** with the **woman** you love...

Comment

Traditional Bibles use the blessed words **live joyfully** by contrast to the hedonistic, secular admonition to **enjoy life**, in most Contemporary Bibles. In Traditional Bibles, the preacher of Ecclesiastes recognizes and celebrates the unique and blessed status of traditional marriage together with its joyful potential. The difference between living with one's wife and living with a woman you love is obvious. The Bible is devoid of God's blessing on *live-in* arrangements, which violate over 3,000 years of Jewish-Christian values and morals.

17

Isaiah 7:14

AV	Behold, a **virgin** shall conceive and bear a Son...
D-R	Behold a **virgin** shall conceive, and bear a son...
KJ21	Behold, a **virgin** shall conceive and bear a Son...
TMB	Behold, a **virgin** shall conceive and bear a Son...

CEV	A **virgin** is pregnant; she will have a son...
GW	A **virgin** will become pregnant and give birth to a son...
NAB	...the **virgin** shall be with child, and bear a son...
NASBU	Behold, a **virgin** will be with child and bear a son...
NIV	The **virgin** will be with child and will give birth to a son...
NJB	...the **young woman** is with child and will give birth to a son...
NKJ	Behold, the **virgin** shall conceive and bear a Son...
NLT	Look! The **virgin** will conceive a child!
NRSV	Look, the **young woman** is with child and shall bear a son...
REB	A **young woman** is with child, and she will give birth to a son...
TEV	...a **young woman** who is pregnant will have a son...

Comment

Here is a monumental difference between the Traditional Bibles and some Contemporary Bibles. A reading of this verse in context discloses the writer's intention to describe a notable and astonishing miracle, namely, the birth of a child to a virgin. But some modern versions substitute the words **young woman** for **virgin**, thereby tending to deprive the birth of our Lord of its miraculous and blessed nature.

The translating of this verse in some Contemporary Bibles is a prime example of the materialist and secularist challenge to the whole concept of the miraculous. In its ancient form this verse is prophetic of the birth of Christ. Changing it is an attack on miracles generally, but more specifically upon the divine birth of our Lord.

Is this deviation from Traditional Bibles consistent with wide-spread efforts of secularists and atheists to explain biblical miracles in terms of natural phenomena?

Isaiah 42:1

AV	...he shall bring forth **judgment** to the Gentiles.
D-R	...he shall bring forth **judgment** to the Gentiles.
KJ21	...He shall bring forth **judgment** to the Gentiles.
TMB	...He shall bring forth **judgment** to the Gentiles.

CEV	...and he will bring **justice** to the nations.
GW	He will bring **justice** to the nations.
NAB	...he shall bring forth **justice** to the nations...
NASBU	...He will bring forth **justice** to the nations.
NIV	...he will bring **justice** to the nations.
NJB	...he will bring fair **judgment** to the nations.
NKJ	...He will bring forth **justice** to the Gentiles.
NLT	He will reveal **justice** to the nations.
NRSV	...he will bring forth **justice** to the nations.
REB	...he will establish **justice** among the nations.
TEV	...he will bring **justice** to every nation.

Comment

This illustrates a recurring difference between Traditional Bibles and Contemporary Bibles. The word **judgment** suggests a distinction between what is morally right and wrong, a concept not favored by modern secular society. The meaning of **justice** in today's parlance has been distorted and diminished to mean social, as distinguished from personal, **justice**. Social justice has come to mean whatever politicians and social scientists want it to mean, often far removed from the righteous **judgment** of God. It is interesting to note that **judgment** appears 294 times in the AV, 132 times in the NIV, and 155 times in the NRSV.

Isaiah 59:9

AV	Therefore is **judgment** far from us, neither doth **justice** overtake us...
D-R	Therefore is **judgment** far from us, and **justice** shall not overtake us.
KJ21	Therefore is **judgment** far from us, neither doth **justice** overtake us...
TMB	Therefore is **judgment** far from us, neither doth **justice** overtake us...

CEV	No one has come to defend us or to bring about **justice**.
GW	...**justice** is far from us, And **righteousness**...
NAB	...**right** is far from us and **justice** does not reach us.
NASBU	...**justice** is far from us, and **righteousness**...
NIV	...**justice** is far from us, and **righteousness**...
NJB	...**judgement** is remote from us nor can **uprightness**...
NKJ	...**justice** is far from us, Nor does **righteousness**...
NLT	...**deliverance** is far from us. That is why God doesn't **punish** those who injure us.
NRSV	Therefore **justice** is far from us, and **righteousness**...
REB	...**justice** is far removed from us, and **righteousness**...
TEV	"Now we know why God does not **save us from those who oppress us.**"

Comment

The above verse is another example of the constantly recurring propensity of the "politically correct" to avoid the use of the word **judgment** in their translations, substituting **justice** instead. Traditional Bibles reflect the profound difference between **judgment** and **justice**. Here the prophet Isaiah demonstrates the fundamental difference between the two by using both words in the same sentence. Translating in a way to blur the difference between **judgment** and **justice** is simply another case among many wherein Contemporary Bibles solidly embrace the no fault—no sin—no judgment concept which permeates modern thinking and contributes to the breakdown of the moral and social values of 3,000 years of Jewish-Christian civilization.

Isaiah 61:1

AV	...to preach good tidings unto the **meek**...
D-R	...he hath sent me to preach to the **meek**...
KJ21	...to preach good tidings unto the **meek**.
TMB	...to preach good tidings unto the **meek**.

CEV	...to tell the **oppressed** the good news...
GW	...to deliver good news to **humble** people.
NAB	He has sent me to bring glad tidings to the **lowly**...
NASBU	...To bring good news to the **afflicted**...
NIV	...to preach good news to the **poor**.
NJB	He has sent me to bring the news to the **afflicted**...
NKJ	...To preach good tidings to the **poor**...
NLT	...to bring good news to the **poor**.
NRSV	...to bring good news to the **oppressed**...
REB	...to announce good news to the **humble**...
TEV	...To bring good news to the **poor**...

Comment

Traditional Bibles speak directly of preaching good tidings to the **meek**; not to the **lowly**, or **afflicted**, or **poor**, or **oppressed**. It is the intention of traditional translators to ascribe God's blessings to the meek, meekness being a blessed quality of the spirit. Contrariwise, it is the inclination of Contemporary Bibles to speak of good tidings to the poor, once again focusing attention on an economic status rather than a spiritual disposition. This is another illustration of the unbiblical adulation of and favoritism for the poor solely on the basis of economic circumstances.

We are all called to deal compassionately with the poor; but contemporary translators adulate the poor as poor, endowing them automatically with virtue, and thereby placing the rich and the poor in class conflict with each other. Lamentably, modern translations often reflect a Hegelian-Marxist, oppressor-oppressed understanding of history which breeds divisiveness, rather than a Father-Son, caring Christian paradigm which emphasizes love and unity.

Jeremiah 8:10

AV ...for every one from the least even unto the greatest is given to **covetousness**...

D-R ...because from the least even to the greatest all follow **covetousness**...

KJ21 For every one from the least even unto the greatest is given to **covetousness**...

TMB For every one from the least even unto the greatest is given to **covetousness**...

CEV Everyone is **greedy** and dishonest, whether poor or rich.

GW All of them, from the least important to the most important, are eager to **make money dishonestly**.

NAB Small and great alike, all are **greedy for gain**...

NASBU ...from the least even to the greatest everyone is **greedy for gain**...

NIV From the least to the greatest, all are **greedy for gain**...

NJB ...from the least to greatest, they are all **greedy for gain**...

NKJ ...from the least even to the greatest everyone is given to **covetousness**...

NLT From the least to the greatest, they trick others to **get what does not belong to them.**

NRSV ...from the least to the greatest everyone is **greedy for unjust gain**...

REB For all, high and low, are out for **ill-gotten gain**;

TEV Everyone, great and small, **tries to make money dishonestly**.

Comment

Covetousness is an inordinate desire to acquire the possessions of another, and is a synonym for the word **envy**. This verse, together with Jeremiah 51:13 and numerous other verses in the Bible, illustrates a distortion in Contemporary Bibles by the substitution of the word **greed**, or variations of it, for the idea of covetousness (envy). Covetousness and envy are words that are anathema to the self-styled architects of contemporary political culture. Hence a word is substituted which cloaks the nature of their political agenda. The substituted word is **greed**. Thus by the use of subtle linguistic manipulation, Bible readers' attention is directed away from the evil of **covetousness** (envy) and toward the evil of **greed**.

Substitution of the word **greed** for the word **covetousness** is a favorite eisegetical ploy of currently dominant social engineers in all of their propaganda and outreach.

Classic Jewish-Christian theology recognizes both **covetousness** (envy) and **greed** as deadly sins, and abominates both equally. But today the political manipulators associate the manifestation of **greed** with normal inclination of all people to better themselves by participating in the economic creative process. These same people neatly and conveniently use the appeal to envy and covetousness as weapons of political control, sowing envy and covetousness whenever possible to divide economic classes, and turn divisiveness into a vehicle for acquiring political power.

What is the result of all of this in modern Bible translations? When the word **covetousness** appears in Traditional Bibles, the word is usually mistranslated in modern versions as **greed**, thereby shifting the focus away from a personal moral fault to a perceived social evil which is wrongfully considered to be inherent in the market process.

Ezekiel 3:19

AV	...but thou hast **delivered thy soul.**
D-R	...but thou hast **delivered thy soul.**
KJ21	...but thou hast **delivered thy soul.**
TMB	...but thou hast **delivered thy soul.**

CEV	...and you will be **innocent.**
GW	...but you will **save yourself.**
NAB	...but you shall **save your life.**
NASBU	...but you have **delivered yourself.**
NIV	...but you will have **saved yourself.**
NJB	...but you yourself will have **saved your life.**
NKJ	...but you have **delivered your soul.**
NLT	But you will have **saved your life** because you did what you were told to do.
NRSV	...but you will have **saved your life.**
REB	...but you will have **discharged your duty.**
TEV	...but your **life will be spared.**

Comment

This verse is an illustration of the profoundly eisegetical efforts of contemporary translators to deny the spiritual concept of **soul** and substitute the gnostic and materialistic concept of *body* or its derivative.

The **soul** is an entity which cannot be scientifically weighed, measured, observed or analyzed, and is therefore ignored by materialists and secularists.

Contemporary translators employ word changes of this sort to justify their claims to superior translating skills. However such changes are not the result of superior translating skills, but reflect clearly the political and social bias of the translators and of the times.

Hosea 10:12

AV	...reap in **mercy**...
D-R	...and reap in the mouth of **mercy**...
KJ21	...reap in **mercy**...
TMB	...reap in **mercy**...

CEV	...and harvest **faithfulness**.
GW	...harvest the fruit that your **loyalty will produce for me**.
NAB	...reap the fruit **of piety**...
NASBU	...Reap in accordance **with kindness**...
NIV	...reap the fruit of **unfailing love**...
NJB	...reap a harvest of **faithful love**...
NKJ	...Reap in **mercy**...
NLT	...harvest a crop of **my love**.
NRSV	...reap **steadfast love**...
REB	...reap **loyalty**.
TEV	...reap the **blessings** that your **devotion** to me will produce.

Comment

Here is an illustration of the aversion of contemporary translators to the word **mercy,** which embodies both the concepts of man's sinfulness and God's forgiveness through the Cross.

A current and virulent example of this rejection is the opposition that many religious leaders are mounting against the whole idea of atonement through the Cross.

We need to be reminded that the word **mercy** in both the Hebrew and English language has a very special significance for both Jews and Christians. The 1828 Webster dictionary reads, "there is perhaps no word in our language precisely synonymous with the word mercy." Webster indicates that **mercy** encompasses the elements of forbearance, benevolence, mildness, tenderness, grace, pity, compassion, charity, clemency, bounty, and forgiveness. Its breadth and depth, and its soulful, loving connotations make it particularly precious for retention in the biblical text.

Note that **mercy** appears 276 times in the AV; 129 times in the NIV; and 138 times in the NRSV.

Bible Word Comparison
Apocrypha/Deuterocanonical Books

(Note: The KJ21 and the Contemporary Bibles which do
not contain the Apocrypha/Deuterocanonical Books
are not included in this section.)

Ecclesiasticus 13:14

D-R   (vs 18) Love God all thy life, and call upon him for thy
salvation.

AV   Love the Lord all thy life, and call upon him for thy
salvation.

TMB   Love the Lord all thy life, and call upon Him for thy
salvation.

NAB   (omitted)
NJB   (omitted)
NRSV   (omitted)
REB   (omitted)
TEV   (omitted)

Comment

In Contemporary Bibles the verse numbering goes from
Eccl. 13:13 to Eccl. 13:15. What happened to verse 14?
Many of God's promises of great solace and comfort have
been omitted from Contemporary Bibles.

Ecclesiasticus 21:27

AV   When the ungodly curseth **Satan**, he curseth **his own soul**.

D-R   (vs 30)While the ungodly curseth the **devil**, he curseth **his own soul**.

TMB   When the ungodly curseth **Satan**, he curseth **his own soul**.

NAB   When a godless man curses **his adversary**, he really curses **himself**.

NJB   When the godless curses **Satan**, he is cursing **himself**.

NRSV   When an ungodly person curses **an adversary**, he curses **himself**.

REB   When the ungodly curses **his adversary**, he is really cursing **himself**.

TEV   When a wicked man curses **his enemy** he is cursing **himself**.

Comment

Traditional Bibles attempt to show a wicked person's similarity to, and affinity with, **Satan** (the devil). Several Contemporary Bibles however attempt to suggest a wicked person's similarity to, and affinity with, his earthly enemy—quite a different message. Thus, what Traditional Bibles regard as a material/spiritual comparison, in Contemporary Bibles turns out to be merely material and secular. Traditional Bibles tend to emphasize transcendental conceptualizations. Contemporary Bibles tend to emphasize present worldly concepts.

28

Ecclesiasticus 26:15

AV   A **shamefaced and faithful woman** is a double grace...
D-R   (19) A **holy and shamefaced woman** is grace upon grace.
TMB   A **shamefaced and faithful woman** is a double grace...

NAB   Choicest of blessings is a **modest wife**...
NJB   A **modest wife** is a boon twice over...
NRSV   A **modest wife** adds charm to charm...
REB   A **modest wife** has infinite charm...
TEV   A **modest wife** has endless charm...

Comment

Traditional Bibles differ from Contemporary Bibles in their attitudes toward the beautiful and soulful word **shamefaced**. It is a much stronger word than **modest**, and is approximately equal in colloquial language to "extremely modest," or perhaps "very modest indeed." By rejecting the word **shamefaced** Contemporary Bibles have settled for a lower level of semantic intensity, with consequent loss of eloquence and power to move the hearts and souls of readers. Where a less intense word is used, the dramatic power of the language is diminished.

In the present example, why did the contemporary Bible translators select **modest** instead of the historic word **shamefaced**? Because the idea of a modern woman being extremely modest or **shamefaced** is incompatible with such characteristics as aggressiveness and confrontationalism, and feeling good about yourself—characteristics popular with contemporary secular culture. A **shamefaced** woman is an affront to a culture of brazenness and aggressiveness.

I Maccabees 3:6

AV	...because **salvation** prospered in his hand.
D-R	...and **salvation** prospered in his hand
TMB	...because **salvation** prospered in his hand.

NAB	By his hand **redemption** was happily achieved...
NJB	...and **deliverance** went forward under his leadership.
NRSV	...and **deliverance** prospered by his hand.
REB	...while the **cause of freedom** prospered in his hands.
TEV	He advanced the **cause of freedom** by what he did.

Comment

Salvation, redemption, deliverance, and **freedom** are all different words with different meanings. Are modern translators so careless in the use of words that they fail to perceive the distinctive meaning involved in the use of each? Is this what is meant by translating by "thought clusters" rather than the formal word-for-word translation used in the historic Bibles?

Note that in their search for the amorphous concept of *meaning*, rather than reflecting the actual *text*, the contemporary translators cannot agree on the specific language to be used. On the other hand, Traditional Bibles are in substantial agreement with each other on such matters.

I Maccabees 9:10

AV   If our time be come, let us die **manfully** for our brethren...

D-R   ...But if our time be come, let us die **manfully** for our brethren...

TMB   If our time be come, let us die **manfully** for our brethren...

NAB   If our time has come, let us die **bravely** for our kinsman...

NJB   If our time has come, at least let us die **like men** for our countrymen...

NRSV If our time has come, let us die **bravely** for our kindred...

REB   ...if our time has come, let us die **bravely** for our fellow countrymen...

TEV   If our time has come, let's die **bravely** for our fellow Jews...

Comment

It appears that certain political groups, in their efforts to promote a gender-neutral culture, object to the attribution of the quality of **manliness** to a soldier, even though the meaning is well understood. This is an example of the constantly recurring linguistic bias in Contemporary Bibles against masculine characterizations.

Bible Word Comparison
New Testament

Matthew 1:25

AV   And knew her not till she had brought forth her
       firstborn son.

D-R   And he knew her not till she brought forth her **firstborn
       son...**

KJ21   ...and knew her not until she had brought forth her **first-
       born Son.**

TMB   ...and knew her not until she had brought forth her **first-
       born Son.**

CEV   But they did not sleep together before her **baby** was
       born.

GW   He did not have marital relations with her before she
       gave birth to **a son.**

NAB   He had no relations with her until she bore **a son...**

NASBU ...but kept her a virgin until she gave birth to **a Son...**

NIV   But he had no union with her until she gave birth to **a
       son.**

NJB   ...he had not had intercourse with her when she gave
       birth to **a son...**

NKJ   ...and did not know her till she had brought forth her
       firstborn Son.

NLT   ...but she remained a virgin until her **son** was born.

NRSV   ...but had no marital relations with her until she had
       borne **a son...**

OxI   ...but he had no marital relations with Mary until she
       had borne **a child...**

REB   ...had no intercourse with her until her **son** was born.

TEV   But he had no sexual relations with her before she gave
       birth to her **son.**

Comment
Traditional Bibles describe Jesus as **firstborn**, but
this specific and important wording has been omitted
from most modern translations. The description of the
virgin birth of our Lord as involving Mary's firstborn
son, has been the essence of the Christian tradition for
over 1900 years. Only in the last half of our sullied
twentieth century has it been challenged.

Matthew 6:13a

AV	And lead us not into **temptation**...
D-R	And lead us not into **temptation**.
KJ21	And lead us not into **temptation**...
TMB	And lead us not into **temptation**...

CEV	Keep us from being **tempted**...
GW	Don't allow us to be **tempted**.
NAB	...and do not subject us to **the final test**...
NASBU	And do not lead us into **temptation**...
NIV	And lead us not into **temptation**...
NJB	And do not put us **to the test**...
NKJ	And do not lead us into **temptation**...
NLT	And don't let us yield to **temptation**...
NRSV	And do not bring us to **the time of trial**...
OxI	And do not bring us to **the time of trial**...
REB	And do not put us **to the test**...
TEV	Do not bring us to **hard testing**...

Comment

Temptation is a word in disfavor with modern secularists, as it focuses attention on the prevalence of sin. But sin is a primary concern to Christ. This is illustrated by Christ's further petition to "deliver us from evil." The **tests, testing,** and **times of trial** alluded to in Contemporary Bibles do not specifically and necessarily focus on moral issues, but could refer to testing as a result of accidents, misfortunes, tragedies, confrontations and trials of a secular nature not necessarily related to the moral circumstances of the petitioner.

Matthew 6:13b

AV	...but **deliver us from evil**...
D-R	But **deliver us from evil**.
KJ21	...but **deliver us from evil**.
TMB	...but **deliver us from evil**.

CEV	...and **protect us from evil**.
GW	Instead, **rescue us from the evil one**.
NAB	...but **deliver us from the evil one**.
NASBU	...but **deliver us from evil**.
NIV	...but **deliver us from the evil one**.
NJB	...but **save us from the Evil One**.
NKJ	But **deliver us from the evil one**.
NLT	...but **deliver us from the evil one**.
NRSV	...but **rescue us from the evil one**.
OxI	...but **rescue us from the evil one**.
REB	...but **save us from the evil one**.
TEV	...but **keep us safe from the Evil One**.

Comment

The focus of Traditional Bibles is introspective, i.e., delivery from the evil in the penitent's own sinful heart. By contrast, in most Contemporary Bibles prayers are directed to deliverance from another who threatens an unspecified harm to the petitioner. The modern renderings tend to de-emphasize the sort of prayer which focuses on the evil residing in the penitent's own heart.

Matthew 11:29

AV	...for I am **meek and lowly** in heart...
D-R	...because I am **meek, and humble** of heart...
KJ21	...for I am **meek and lowly** in heart...
TMB	...for I am **meek and lowly** in heart...

CEV	I am **gentle and humble**...
GW	...because I am **gentle and humble**.
NAB	...for I am **meek and humble** of heart...
NASBU	...for I am **gentle and humble** in heart...
NIV	...for I am **gentle and humble** in heart...
NJB	...for I am **gentle and humble** in heart...
NKJ	...for I am **gentle and lowly** in heart...
NLT	...because I am **humble and gentle**...
NRSV	...for I am **gentle and humble** in heart...
OxI	...for I am **gentle and humble** in heart...
REB	...for I am **gentle and humble**-hearted...
TEV	...because I am **gentle and humble** in spirit...

Comment

In the Traditional Bibles, Christ describes Himself as meek and lowly. But in our modern age, which lays great stress on such matters as self-assertiveness, one-up-manship and egoistical introspection, the words **meek** and **lowly** are in great disfavor.

There are many examples in Contemporary Bibles which reflect distaste for certain powerful words which the Traditional Bibles routinely use. See for example the aversion to the word **shamefaced** found in Ecclesiasticus 26:15.

Matthew 16:16

AV	And Simon Peter answered and said, Thou art the **Christ**...
D-R	Simon Peter answered and said: Thou art **Christ**...
KJ21	And Simon Peter answered and said, "Thou art the **Christ**...
TMB	And Simon Peter answered and said, "Thou art the **Christ**...

CEV	Simon Peter spoke up, "You are the **Messiah**...
GW	Simon Peter answered, "You are the **Messiah**...
NAB	Simon Peter said in reply, "You are the **Messiah**...
NASBU	Simon Peter answered, "You are the **Christ**...
NIV	Simon Peter answered, "You are the **Christ**...
NJB	Then Simon Peter spoke up and said, 'You are the **Christ**...
NKJ	...Simon Peter answered and said, "You are the **Christ**...
NLT	Simon Peter answered, "You are the **Messiah**...
NRSV	Simon Peter answered, "You are the **Messiah**...
OxI	Simon Peter answered, "You are the **Messiah**...
REB	Simon Peter answered: 'You are the **Messiah**...
TEV	Simon Peter answered, "You are the **Messiah**...

Comment

Note the difference among translations in respect to the enormously important understanding of the nature of Christ Himself. Most traditional and conservative translators use the word **Christ**, whereas the word **Messiah** is used by most contemporary translators.

We pose this question: is the difference in word selection due to relative skill in translating, or social and theological bias? **Messiah** is a historically Hebrew concept and describes a much awaited and anticipated hero-figure who would deliver Israel from its political oppressors and had been prophesied by Hebrew prophets for hundreds of years before Christ. The **Messiah** was historically not endowed with the power to forgive sins. The word **Christ** is a more complete and adequate description of Jesus, the Son of God who came to save the entire world from its sins, and who also forgives sins. Hebrew and Greek scholars tell us that the Jewish concept of **Messiah** did not include viewing Jesus as *God* (Oeos).

Matthew 17:21

AV	**Howbeit this kind goeth not out but by prayer and fasting.**
D-R	**(vs 20)But this kind is not cast out but by prayer and fasting.**
KJ21	**...this kind goeth not out but by prayer and fasting.**"
TMB	**...this kind goeth not out but by prayer and fasting.**"

CEV	omitted
GW	omitted
NAB	omitted
NASBU	[**"But this kind does not go out except by prayer and fasting.**"]
NIV	omitted
NJB	omitted
NKJ	**"However, this kind does not go out except by prayer and fasting.**"
NLT	omitted
NRSV	omitted
OxI	omitted
REB	omitted
TEV	omitted

Comment

A striking difference between Traditional Bibles and the contemporary group is the astonishing number of words in the traditional translations which are entirely omitted in Contemporary Bibles. It has been calculated that there are almost 3,000 fewer words in the New Testament alone in Contemporary Bibles than in Traditional Bibles. The question arises: who decided to leave these words out? By what authority? To what end? For what reason? The answer is: these and numerous other omissions are the result of contemporary translators' use of a deficient New Testament Greek text. Traditional translations are based on the Byzantine (Ecclesiastical) Text, which is reflected in more than 5,000 ancient manuscripts; whereas modern translations are based on the Alexandrian cluster of texts, of which only a handful of ancient manuscripts are still in existence. Ignored and unused for over 1500 years, the Alexandrian Texts were first used as the basis for an English Bible translation in 1881.

Matthew 28:19

AV	...baptizing them in the name of the Father, and of the Son, and of the **holy Ghost**.
D-R	...baptizing them in the name of the Father, and of the Son, and of the **Holy Ghost**.
KJ21	...baptizing them in the name of the Father, and of the Son, and of the **Holy Spirit**.
TMB	...baptizing them in the name of the Father, and of the Son, and of the **Holy Ghost**.

CEV	Baptize them in the name of the Father, the Son, and the **Holy Spirit**.
GW	...baptize them in the name of the Father, and of the Son, and of the **Holy Spirit**.
NAB	...baptizing them in the name of the Father, and of the Son, and of the **holy Spirit**.
NASBU	...baptizing them in the name of the Father and the Son and the **Holy Spirit**...
NIV	...baptizing them in the name of the Father and of the Son and of the **Holy Spirit**.
NJB	...baptise them in the name of the Father and of the Son, and of the **Holy Spirit**...
NKJ	...baptizing them in the name of the Father and of the Son and of the **Holy Spirit**...
NLT	...baptizing them in the name of the Father and the Son and the **Holy Spirit**.
NRSV	...baptizing them in the name of the Father and of the Son and of the **Holy Spirit**...
OxI	...baptizing them in the name of the Father-Mother and of the beloved Child and of the **Holy Spirit**...
REB	...baptize them in the name of the Father and the Son and the Holy **Spirit**...
TEV	...baptizing them in the name of the Father, the Son, and the Holy **Spirit**...

Comment

Holy Spirit or **Holy Ghost**? Which is better? Neither term is obsolete or archaic. Neither is incorrect. Unabridged dictionaries, including the great *Webster's New International Dictionary*, Second Edition Unabridged, always define **Holy Ghost** as the third person of the Trinity. Most modern unabridged dictionaries define **Holy Spirit** as God present and active in human experience, and some also give it a secondary meaning, namely, **Holy Ghost**. The two great historical Bibles use **Holy Ghost** as being more perfectly reflective of the ancient and venerable Ecclesiastical (canonical) Text.

There are other reasons why the term **Holy Ghost** is to be preferred to **Holy Spirit**: it conveys a greater sense of awe, mystery, and holiness. It more clearly differentiates the third person of the Godhead from the less exactly perceived, and more generalized, spirit of God. Also and importantly, **Holy Ghost** is less subject to being distorted by New Age socio-linguists into an impersonal, generalized *force* in the universe rather than a personal God. **Holy Ghost** therefore more graphically affirms the orthodox concept of the Holy Trinity, whereas **Holy Spirit** is more easily adaptable to secularist, modernist, and atheistic conceptualizations. New Age socio-linguists are always seeking to remold Christian orthodoxy to their own preferences and thought processes. The term **Holy Spirit** presents a better target for secular linguistic distortion than does **Holy Ghost**.

Note that in the Traditional Bibles **Holy Ghost** is used in the New Testament approximately 87 times; **Holy Spirit** is used once in the New Testament; **holy Spirit** is used three times, and **the Spirit** is used 125 times. Traditional Bibles thus possess a linguistic selectivity and refinement which tends to be lost in Contemporary Bibles.

Mark 5:30

AV   And Jesus, immediately knowing in himself that **virtue** had gone out of him...

D-R   And immediately Jesus knowing in himself the **virtue** that had proceeded from him...

KJ21 And Jesus, immediately knowing in Himself that **virtue** had gone out of Him...

TMB   And Jesus, immediately knowing in Himself that **virtue** had gone out of Him...

CEV   At that moment Jesus felt **power** go out from him.

GW   At that moment Jesus felt **power** had gone out of him.

NAB   Jesus, aware at once that **power** had gone out from him...

NASBU Immediately Jesus, perceiving in Himself that the **power** proceeding from Him had gone forth...

NIV   At once Jesus realized that **power** had gone out from him.

NJB   And at once aware of the **power** that had gone out from him...

NKJ   And Jesus, immediately knowing in Himself that **power** had gone out of Him...

NLT   Jesus realized at once that **healing power** had gone out from him...

NRSV Immediately aware that **power** had gone forth from him...

OxI   Immediately aware that **power** had gone forth from him...

REB   Aware at once that **power** had gone out of him...

TEV   At once Jesus knew that **power** had gone out of him...

Comment

In the Traditional Bibles, St. Mark recognizes that Christ's healing qualities come from **virtue** rather than from **power**. **Virtue**, is not a "politically correct" concept, and in our modern secular world the attainment of **power** is the defining aim of the political-economic agenda. The distinction between **virtue** and **power**, as illustrated in this example, reflects a profound disagreement between traditional and modern views as to the dynamic forces at work in the universe. Traditional Bibles speak of the ultimate conflict between good and evil, between virtue and demonism.

41

Modern secular socio-linguists are perfectly willing to relegate this traditional dichotomy to oblivion, preferring to interpret history and social dynamics in terms of power confrontations. Such is the intellectual environment of Hegel and Marx, in which the factor of virtue in explaining historical developments is considered either as irrelevant, or simply non-existent. Thus, to secularists the explanation for a miraculous healing event described here becomes not an exercise of the virtue of Christ, but an exercise of the impersonal force. Moderns would rather view Christ as superman and wonder worker than as the wondrous and humble Suffering Servant.

But consider the totality of the Bible from Genesis to Revelation: is the lesson to be gleaned that power is the ultimate winner however evil it might be, or is it that ultimately the virtue of righteousness is triumphant?

By God's grace and mercy, His virtue, righteousness, and godliness will prevail in the end over all the forces of sin, hatred, power, and evil.

Luke 2:14

AV   ...and on earth peace, **good will towards men.**

D-R   Glory to God in the highest; and on earth peace **to men of good will.**

KJ21   "...and on earth peace, **good will toward men!**"

TMB   "...and on earth peace, **good will toward men!**"

CEV   "Peace on earth **to everyone who pleases God.**"

GW   "...and on earth peace **to those who have his good will!**"

NAB   "... and on earth peace **to those on whom his favor rests.**"

NASBU   "...And on earth peace **among men with whom He is pleased.**"

NIV   "...and on earth peace **to men on whom his favor rests.**"

NJB   ...and on earth peace **for those he favours.**

NKJ   "...And on earth peace, **good will toward men!**"

NLT   "...and peace on earth **to all whom God favors.**"

NRSV   "...and on earth peace **among those whom he favors!**"

OxI   "...and on earth peace **among those with whom God is pleased!**"

REB   "...and on earth peace **to all in whom he delights.**"

TEV   "...and peace on earth **to those with whom he is pleased!**"

Comment

Does the birth of Christ, accompanied by the praise of a multitude of angels, signify a glorious event to be shared by the human race generally, or is it a blessing shared only by and for those who are favored by God and pleasing to Him? Does not the Lord send His rain on the just and the unjust? (Mt 5:45)

43

Luke 2:33

AV	And **Joseph** and his mother marveled...
D-R	And **his father** and mother were wondering...
KJ21	And **Joseph** and His mother marveled...
TMB	And **Joseph** and His mother marveled...

CEV	**Jesus' parents** were surprised...
GW	**Jesus' father** and mother were amazed...
NAB	The **child's father** and mother were amazed...
NASBU	And **His father** and mother were amazed...
NIV	The **child's father** and mother marveled...
NJB	As the **child's father** and mother were wondering...
NKJ	And **Joseph** and His mother marveled...
NLT	**Joseph** and Mary were amazed...
NRSV	And the **child's father** and mother were amazed...
OxI	And **Jesus' father** and mother were amazed...
REB	The **child's father** and mother were full of wonder...
TEV	The **child's father** and mother were amazed...

Comment

Query: Who was the father of Jesus Christ, Joseph or God?

44

Luke 4:4

AV   ...man shall not live by bread alone, **but by every word of God.**

D-R   ...Man liveth not by bread alone, **but by every word of God.**

KJ21   '...Man shall not live by bread alone, **but by every word of God.**'

TMB   '...Man shall not live by bread alone, **but by every word of God.**'

CEV   (omitted)
GW   (omitted)
NAB   (omitted)
NASBU   (omitted)
NIV   (omitted)
NJB   (omitted)
NKJ   'Man shall not live by bread alone, **but by every word of God.**'
NLT   (omitted)
NRSV   (omitted)
OxI   (omitted)
REB   (omitted)
TEV   (omitted)

Comment

Scripture is used to interpret Scripture. Thus, every time a crucial word or statement is left out, biblical teaching is undermined. The opposite is also true, namely, every time the translator leaves in a crucial word or statement, as in versions based on the traditional, canonical Byzantine text, it preserves and reinforces a crucial Christian truth. In this case, the truth is that we serve a God who asks us to live by every word of His revelation.

Also similar omissions from most Contemporary Bibles are Matthew 17:21; 18:11; 23:14; Mark 7:16; 9:44, 46; 11:26; 15:28; 16:9-20; Luke 17:36; 23:17; John 5:4; 7:53-8:11; Acts 8:37; 15:34; 24:7; 28:29; Romans 16:24, to name a few among others.

This particular type of deletion is illustrative not of a translation error but rather of the selection by modern translators of a different, shorter, and inferior text for translation purposes.

45

Luke 9:20

AV	But whom say ye that I am? Peter answering said, **The Christ of God.**
D-R	Simon Peter answering, said: **The Christ of God.**
KJ21	Peter answering said, **"The Christ of God!"**
TMB	Peter answering said, **"The Christ of God!"**

CEV	..."You are **the Messiah sent from God.**"
GW	..."You are **the Messiah, whom God has sent.**"
NAB	..."**The Messiah of God.**"
NASBU	..."**The Christ of God.**"
NIV	..."**The Christ of God.**"
NJB	...'**The Christ of God**'...
NKJ	..."**The Christ of God.**"
NLT	..."You are **the Messiah sent from God!**"
NRSV	..."**The Messiah of God.**"
OxI	..."**The Messiah of God.**"
REB	...'**God's Messiah.**'
TEV	..."You are **God's Messiah.**"

Comment

Is Jesus **the Christ of God** or **the Messiah**? This is an enormously important issue, about which there is wide disagreement. The answer reflects profound theological differences. Note above that all Traditional Bibles are identical, but that a number of the Contemporary Bibles vary both from the Traditional Bibles and from each other.

But consider: can the Messiah forgive sins? **Messiah** is a term which reflects the ancient expectations of the Hebrew people. Fundamentally, the Old Testament describes the Messiah as a leader who would be able to deliver the Israelites from their oppressors here on earth. But Jesus Christ is God Himself in His second person.

Contemporary Bibles, in making reference to **the Christ of God** as **the Messiah**, are departing from the tradition of historic Christendom.

Luke 12:15

AV	Take heed and beware of **covetousness**...
D-R	...Take heed: and beware of all **covetousness**...
KJ21	"Take heed and beware of **covetousness**...
TMB	"Take heed and beware of **covetousness**...

CEV	Don't be **greedy**!
GW	Be careful to guard yourselves from every kind of **greed**.
NAB	Take care to guard against all **greed**...
NASBU	Beware, and be on your guard against every form of **greed**...
NIV	Watch out! Be on your guard against all kinds of **greed**...
NJB	Watch, and be on your guard against **avarice** of any kind...
NKJ	Take heed and beware of **covetousness**...
NLT	Beware! Don't be **greedy** for what you don't have.
NRSV	Take care! Be on your guard against all kinds of **greed**...
OxI	Take care! Be on your guard against all kinds of **greed**...
REB	Beware! Be on your guard against **greed** of every kind...
TEV	...Watch out and guard yourselves from every kind of **greed**...

Comment

Why was the word **covetousness** in the traditional translations changed by modern translators to **greed**? Christ's concern here is with the sinful desire to acquire what belongs to another (covetousness), not with an excessive desire to accumulate wealth (greed). The fostering of feelings of covetousness and envy historically has been used by demagogues to promote class rivalry and conflict for questionable political purposes. Such people greatly favor substituting the word **greed,** which is erroneously used by this same group to characterize the motives of market-oriented activity. Word distortion of this type is the result of translator bias. (For additional discussion, please refer to Jeremiah 8:10.)

Luke 17:19

AV   ...thy faith hath made thee **whole**.
D-R   ...for thy faith hath made thee **whole**.
KJ21   "Thy faith hath made thee **whole**."
TMB   "Thy faith hath made thee **whole**."

CEV   "Your faith has made you **well**."
GW   "Your faith has made you **well**."
NAB   "...your faith has **saved** you."
NASBU "...your faith has made you **well**."
NIV   "...your faith has made you **well**."
NJB   '...Your faith has **saved** you.'
NKJ   "Your faith has made you **well**."
NLT   "Your faith has made you **well**."
NRSV   "...your faith has made you **well**."
OxI   "...your faith has made you **well**."
REB   '...your faith has **cured** you.'
TEV   "...your faith has made you **well**."

Comment

Substitution of the word **well** for the superior and more inclusive word **whole** is an illustration of the attempt by contemporary translators to secularize modern thinking. The word **well** in modern parlance suggests a desirable physical condition, whereas **whole** embodies, more comprehensively, the entire person including the physical, psychological, and spiritual dimensions. The body is made **well**, whereas the totality of the person is made **whole**.

Luke 23:32

AV   And there were also two other **malefactors** led with him, to be put to death.

D-R   ...two other **malefactors** led with him to be put to death.

KJ21 ...two others, **malefactors**, led with Him to be put to death.

TMB   ...two others, **malefactors**, led with Him to be put to death.

CEV   Two **criminals** were led out to be put to death with Jesus.

GW   Two others, who were **criminals**, were led away...

NAB   Now two others, both **criminals**, were led away...

NASBU Two others also, who were **criminals**, were being led...

NIV   Two other men, both **criminals**...

NJB   Now they were also leading out two others, **criminals,** to be executed with him.

NKJ   There were also two others, **criminals**, led with Him...

NLT   Two others, both **criminals**, were led out to be executed...

NRSV Two others also, who were **criminals**, were led away...

OxI   Two others also, who were **criminals**, were led away...

REB   There were two others with him, **criminals** who were...

TEV   Two other men, both of them **criminals**, were also...

Comment

Traditional Bibles characterize the men who were crucified with Christ as **malefactors**. Contemporary Bibles characterized these two men as **criminals**. A **malefactor** is an evil person by definition. A **criminal**, on the other hand, is a person condemned by a ruling judicial and political authority. Not all people who are adjudged **criminals** according to some secular code of law, are **malefactors**, but all malefactors are evil-doers. Conduct which political society defines as criminal is profoundly different from conduct which biblical tradition defines as evil. For example, some political protestors are arrested, convicted and jailed; but they are not necessarily **malefactors**.

The law of right and wrong—God's law—defines who are **malefactors**. The law of political powers defines who are **criminals**, some of whom may be malefactors, and some of whom may be, in fact, heroes and saints.

John 6:69

AV	And we believe and are sure that **thou art that Christ, the Son of the living God.**
D-R	(vs 70) And we have believed and have known, that **thou art the Christ, the Son of God.**
KJ21	"...and we believe and are sure that **Thou art that Christ, the Son of the living God.**"
TMB	"...and we believe and are sure that **Thou art that Christ, the Son of the living God.**"

CEV	"We have faith in you, and we are sure that **you are God's Holy One.**"
GW	"...know that **you are the Holy One of God.**"
NAB	"We have come to believe and are convinced that **you are the Holy One of God.**"
NASBU	"We have believed and have come to know that **You are the Holy One of God.**"
NIV	"We believe and know that **you are the Holy One of God.**"
NJB	'...and we believe; we have come to know that **you are the Holy One of God.**'
NKJ	"Also we have come to believe and know that **You are the Christ, the Son of the living God.**"
NLT	"We believe them, and we know **you are the Holy One of God.**"
NRSV	"We have come to believe and know that **you are the Holy One of God.**"
OxI	"...know that **you are the Holy One of God.**"
REB	'We believe and know that **you are God's Holy One.**'
TEV	"And now we believe and know that **you are the Holy One who has come from God.**"

Comment

The overpowering confession of Peter that Christ is the Son of the Living God is translated quite differently in the majority of Contemporary Bibles from the Traditional Bibles. Plainly put; is Jesus the Christ, the Son of the Living God, or is He something lesser, as suggested in contemporary translations? The overall emphasis in Contemporary Bibles can be interpreted as diminishing the deity of Christ from holy, godly, Trinitarian glory to the status of a worldly-wise and fallible man sent by God to influence people for good.

John 9:35

AV	...he said unto him, Dost thou believe on the **Son of God**?
D-R	...he said to him: Dost thou believe in the **Son of God**?
KJ21	...He said unto him, "Dost thou believe in the **Son of God**?"
TMB	...He said unto him, "Dost thou believe in the **Son of God**?"

CEV	Then Jesus asked, "Do you have faith in the **Son of Man**?"
GW	...he asked him, "Do you believe in the **Son of Man**?"
NAB	...he found him and said, "Do you believe in the **Son of Man**?"
NASBU	...He said, "Do you believe in the **Son of Man**?"
NIV	...he said, "Do you believe in the **Son of Man**?"
NJB	...he said to him, 'Do you believe in the **Son of man**?'
NKJ	...He said to him, "Do you believe in the **Son of God**?"
NLT	...and said, "Do you believe in the **Son of Man**?"
NRSV	...he said, "Do you believe in the **Son of Man**?"
OxI	...he said, "Do you believe in the **Human One**?"
REB	...Jesus found him and asked, 'Have you faith in the **Son of Man**?'
TEV	...and asked him, "Do you believe in the **Son of Man**?"

Comment

The issue raised in the comparison of this verse: Is Christ the **Son of God**, or is he the **Son of Man**? Also note the gross distortion of meaning which occurs as a result of the use of gender-neutral language (Oxford Inclusive Version). There is undeniably a dramatic theological difference in the perception of Christ involved here. Christ is not the **Son of Man** or of any man, but is instead God Himself in the blessed second person of the Holy Trinity.

Acts 2:27

AV	Because thou wilt not leave my soul in **hell**...
D-R	Because thou wilt not leave my soul in **hell**...
KJ21	...because Thou wilt not leave my soul in **hell**...
TMB	...because Thou wilt not leave my soul in **hell**...

CEV	The Lord won't leave me in the **grave**.
GW	...because you do not abandon my soul to the **grave**...
NAB	...because you will not abandon my soul to the **nether world**...
NASBU	Because You will not abandon my soul to **Hades**...
NIV	...because you will not abandon me to the **grave**...
NJB	...for you will not abandon me to **Hades**...
NKJ	Because you will not leave my soul in **Hades**...
NLT	For you will not leave my soul **among the dead**...
NRSV	For you will not abandon my soul to **Hades**...
OxI	For you will not abandon my soul to **Hades**...
REB	...for you will not abandon me to **death**...
TEV	...because you will not abandon me in the **world of the dead**...

Comment

Traditional Bibles use the word **hell**, whereas Contemporary Bibles use various euphemistic wordings. In all Traditional Bibles **hell** is a place or a circumstance of punishment in the afterlife. The whole concept of sinful people being punished is anathema to a modern, morally-neutral culture, the rationale being that deviant moral conduct is a product of social environment and therefore not the fault of the person committing the act. Thereby society is made responsible for evil deeds, and individuals become victims and therefore should not be considered sinners. This illustration is representative of alterations made in the ancient Greek manuscripts which reflect the theological agenda of an early heretical group associated with the city of Alexandria, known as Gnostics. Modern day Gnostics of various stripes embrace these inferior Alexandrian texts used as the basis for many Contemporary Bibles.

Acts 8:37

AV   ...I believe that Jesus Christ is the Son of God.

D-R   ...I believe that Jesus Christ is the Son of God.

KJ21   ..."I believe that Jesus Christ is the Son of God."

TMB   ..."I believe that Jesus Christ is the Son of God."

CEV   (omitted)
GW   (omitted)
NAB   (omitted)
NASBU   ..."I believe that Jesus Christ is the Son of God."
NIV   (omitted)
NJB   (omitted)
NKJ   ..."I believe that Jesus Christ is the Son of God."
NLT   (omitted)
NRSV   (omitted)
OxI   (omitted)
REB   (omitted)
TEV   (omitted)

Comment

Notice that here all Traditional Bibles, and also the conservative Contemporary Bibles, contain the ringing confession and affirmation of the Ethiopian official that Christ is the Son of God. But most modern translators either omit this clause entirely or put it in a footnote implying that only lesser versions contain it. Such is yet another example of omissions in Contemporary Bibles resulting from the translators' use of the shorter Alexandrian cluster of Greek texts. It has been suggested previously in this discussion that the Alexandrian Text, the basis for almost all modern translations, is the product of editing by early Gnostic sects in order to conform Scripture to suit their particular heretical theological agenda. It requires no stretch of the imagination to conclude that the affirmation that **Jesus Christ is the Son of God,** as found in traditional versions, would hardly suit such an agenda.

Acts 10:34

AV   Then Peter opened his mouth, and said ...God is **no respecter of persons**...

D-R   And Peter opening his mouth, said...and God is **not a respecter of persons**.

KJ21   Then Peter opened his mouth and said "...God is **no respecter of persons**..."

TMB   Then Peter opened his mouth and said ...God is **no respecter of persons**...

CEV   Peter then said: Now I am certain that God **treats all people alike**.

GW   Then Peter said, "Now I understand that God **doesn't play favorites**."

NAB   Then Peter proceeded to speak and said, "In truth, I see that God **shows no partiality**."

NASBU   Opening his mouth, Peter said: "I most certainly understand now that God is **not one to show partiality**..."

NIV   Then Peter began to speak: "...God **does not show favoritism**..."

NJB   Then Peter addressed them, '...God **has no favourites**...'

NKJ   Then Peter opened his mouth and said: "...God **shows no partiality**."

NLT   Then Peter replied, "I see very clearly that God **doesn't show partiality**."

NRSV   Then Peter began to speak to them: "I truly understand that God **shows no partiality**,"

OxI   Then Peter began to speak to them: "...God **shows no partiality**..."

REB   Peter began: "...God **has no favourites**,"

TEV   Peter began to speak: "I now realize that it is true that God **treats everyone on the same basis**."

Comment

Contemporary Bibles are the source of one of the great errors of modern secularists. This passage in Traditional Bibles indicates that God does not show favor on the basis of worldly status (i.e., social, economic, cultural or political status of people). It makes no difference whether people are poor or rich, weak or powerful, male or female, or of any particular color of skin. Contemporary Bibles, on the other hand, say that God has no favorites and treats all people alike. This, of course, is utterly untrue. A recurring message of the Bible from Genesis to Revelation is that God does in fact have His favorites, namely, His children who sincerely love Him, earnestly try to live by His Word, keep His commandments, and receive His Son as Savior and God. The implication of modern translations, on the other hand, is clear: it doesn't make any difference how a person lives or how grossly he defies God's law; such a person shares God's favor equally with persons who love Him and live in accordance with His laws.

Historic Bibles reflect this seminal theme: God has a preference for the good—not a preference for the poor or the rich, or the weak or the powerful. God's preference extends to virtuous and godly people, regardless of their race, national origin, color, or economic circumstance.

Romans 13:1

AV	Let every soul be subject unto the **higher powers**...
D-R	Let every soul be subject to **higher**...
KJ21	Let every soul be subject unto the **higher**...
TMB	Let every soul be subject unto the **higher**...

CEV	Only God can give **authority** to anyone, and he puts these **rulers** in their places of power.
GW	Every person should obey the **government** in power.
NAB	Let every person be subordinate to the **higher authorities**...
NASBU	Every person is to be in subjection to the **governing authorities**...
NIV	Everyone must submit himself to the **governing authorities**...
NJB	Everyone is to obey the **governing authorities**...
NKJ	Let every soul be subject to the **governing authorities**...
NLT	Obey the **government**, for God is the one who put it there.
NRSV	Let every person be subject to the **governing authorities**...
OxI	Let every person be subject to the **governing authorities**...
REB	Every person must submit to the **authorities in power**...
TEV	Everyone must obey **state authorities**...

Comment

Note that, by contrast with Traditional Bibles, Contemporary Bibles equate **higher powers** solely with governmental powers.

While the term **higher powers** as used in Traditional Bibles may refer to governing authorities, more importantly it carries reference to godly spiritual forces, encompassing our mighty Trinitarian God Himself and His unseen and limitless force of angels and saints.

This verse, as it appears in most Contemporary Bibles, is often used to justify subservience and obedience to all government dictates, no matter how evil or ungodly.

Romans 16:1

AV	...Phebe our sister, which is a **servant** of the church...
D-R	...Phebe, our sister, who is in the **ministry** of the church...
KJ21	...Phoebe our sister, who is a **servant** of the church...
TMB	...Phoebe our sister, who is a **servant** of the church...

CEV	...Phoebe, who is a **leader** in the church...
GW	...Phoebe to you. She is our sister in the Christian faith and a **deacon** of the church...
NAB	...Phoebe our sister, who is [also] a **minister** of the church...
NASBU	...Phoebe, who is a **servant** of the church...
NIV	...Phoebe, a **servant** of the church...
NJB	...Phoebe, a **deaconess** of the church...
NKJ	...Phoebe our sister, who is a **servant** of the church...
NLT	...Phoebe, a **deacon** in the church...
NRSV	...Phoebe, a **deacon** of the church...
OxI	...Phoebe, a **deacon** of the church...
REB	...Phoebe, a fellow-Christian who is a **minister** in the church...
TEV	...Phoebe, who **serves** the church...

Comment

Servanthood is identified in the Gospel as the highest and most laudable form of all interpersonal relationships ("But he that is greatest among you shall be your servant." Mt. 23:11). But most modern translators are loath to suggest that servanthood should apply to womankind. Servanthood, in the modern view, represents an abandonment of a principal aim of modern womanhood, the attainment of power; hence a different word must be found more compatible with the secular agenda. Submissiveness and servanthood, qualities of character manifested in the life of our Lord, have fallen out of favor in a world which increasingly becomes secularized in character, and where people have become more self-centered in personal orientation. Servanthood as an admirable trait has been supplanted by a passionate quest for personal pleasure and feeling good about oneself.

1 Corinthians 7:3

AV	Let the husband render unto the wife **due benevolence**...
D-R	Let the husband render the **debt** to his wife...
KJ21	Let the husband render unto the wife **due benevolence**...
TMB	Let the husband render unto the wife **due benevolence**...

CEV	Husbands and wives **should be fair with each other about having sex.**
GW	Husbands and wives **should satisfy each other's sexual needs.**
NAB	The husband should **fulfill his duty** toward his wife...
NASBU	The husband must **fulfill his duty** to his wife...
NIV	The husband should **fulfill his marital duty** to his wife...
NJB	The husband must give to his wife **what she has a right to expect**...
NKJ	Let the husband render to his wife **the affection due her**...
NLT	The husband should not deprive his wife of **sexual intimacy**...
NRSV	The husband should give to his wife her **conjugal rights**...
OxI	...husband should give to his wife her **conjugal rights**...
REB	The husband must give the wife **what is due to her**...
TEV	A man should **fulfill his duty** as a husband...

Comment

In the Traditional Bibles St. Paul admonishes husbands to fulfill much more than marital duties, namely, to exhibit to their wives nothing short of **benevolence**. Benevolence, properly understood, connotes the relationship of goodwill, charitableness and love, plus a fervent desire to contribute to another's happiness and well-being. Contemporary Bibles tend to reduce the relationship between husband and wife to a mere balancing of sexual and social duties, rights, and powers. Is it any wonder that the institution of marriage has fallen into such a state of perceived irrelevance in our culture, with consequent disregard for committed and lasting relationships?

1 Corinthians 13:1

AV   Though I speak with the tongues of men and of Angels, and have not **charity**...

D-R   If I speak with the tongues of men, and of angels, and have not **charity**...

KJ21   Though I speak with the tongues of men and of angels, but have not **charity**...

TMB   Though I speak with the tongues of men and of angels, but have not **charity**...

CEV   What if I could speak all languages of humans and of angels? If I did not **love** others...

GW   I may speak in the languages of humans and of angels. But if I don't have **love**...

NAB   If I speak in human and angelic tongues but do not have **love**...

NASBU   If I speak with the tongues of men and of angels, but do not have **love**...

NIV   If I speak in the tongues of men and of angels, but have not **love**...

NJB   Though I command languages both human and angelic —if I speak without **love**...

NKJ   Though I speak with the tongues of men and of angels, but have not **love**...

NLT   If I could speak in any language in heaven or on earth but didn't **love** others...

NRSV   If I speak in the tongues of mortals and of angels, but do not have **love**...

OxI   If I speak in the tongues of mortals and of angels, but do not have **love**...

REB   I may speak in tongues of men or of angels, but if I have no **love**...

TEV   I may be able to speak the languages of men and even of angels, but if I have no **love**...

Comment

In this wonderfully moving and eloquent chapter, the Traditional Bibles are correct in using **charity** instead of **love**. *Webster's New International Dictionary*, Second Edition, Unabridged (Webster II), defines charity with precision: "Christian love; specif.: The virtue or act of loving God with a love which transcends that for creatures, and of loving others for the sake of God;—is

rendered in Greek as *agape* in the New Testament."
The word **love**, though it may connote selflessness, can also mean a number of other things, including brotherly love, romantic love, erotic love, love of country, etc. Charity is the highest form of love, i.e., Christian love (*agape*). There is no precise English word equivalent for the Greek word *agape*. The traditional translators chose **charity** rather than **love** as more precisely meaningful. **Charity** triumphs even over faith and hope.

This is an age devoted to the banalizing, romanticizing, commercial exploitation and perversion of the concept of love. The great traditional translators providentially anticipated this development and provided the best possible translation of the Greek word *agape* in order that the depth and precision of its meaning might not be lost.

2 Corinthians 13:11

AV	Finally, brethren, farewell: **Be perfect...**
D-R	For the rest, brethren, rejoice, **be perfect...**
KJ21	Finally, brethren, farewell. **Be perfect...**
TMB	Finally, brethren, farewell. **Be perfect...**

CEV	Goodby, my friends. **Do better...**
GW	With that, brothers and sisters, I must say goodbye. **Make sure that you improve...**
NAB	Finally, brothers, rejoice. **Mend your ways...**
NASBU	Finally, brethren, rejoice, **be made complete...**
NIV	Finally, brothers, good-by. **Aim for perfection...**
NJB	To end then, brothers, we wish you joy; **try to grow perfect...**
NKJ	Finally, brethren, farewell. **Become complete...**
NLT	Dear friends, I close my letter with these last words: Rejoice. **Change your ways.**
NRSV	Finally, brothers and sisters, farewell. **Put things in order.**
OxI	Finally, sisters and brothers, farewell. **Put things in order.**
REB	And now, my friends, farewell. **Mend your ways...**
TEV	And now, my brothers, goodbye! **Strive for perfection...**

Comment

In the Traditional Bibles (and also the more conservative Contemporary Bibles), St. Paul admonishes his hearers to strive for the highest level of virtue, namely, perfection. Contemporary Bibles fall short in expressing Paul's high standards and ideals. *Are you going on to perfection?*—a question asked many candidates for the ministry—reflects the biblical standard that is satisfied with nothing short of perfection. Perfection should be an aim of every child of God who earnestly desires and works for the Kingdom of God, however unlikely it is to be realized in this life. To use a less powerful word is to downgrade God's standard of perfection.

Ephesians 2:10

AV	For we are **his workmanship**...
D-R	For we are **his workmanship**...
KJ21	For we are **His workmanship**...
TMB	For we are **His workmanship**...

CEV	...sent Christ to **make us what we are.**
GW	God has **made us what we are.**
NAB	For we are **his handiwork.**
NASBU	For we are **His workmanship.**
NIV	For we are **God's workmanship**...
NJB	We are **God's work of art**...
NKJ	For we are **His workmanship**...
NLT	For we are **God's masterpiece.**
NRSV	For we are **what he has made us**...
OxI	For we are **what God has made us**...
REB	...we are **God's handiwork**...
TEV	God has **made us what we are**...

Comment

Is there a difference between describing mankind as a) **His workmanship** and b) **what he has made us**? It is submitted that being called God's workmanship implies that we are created beings made in the image of God. Other translations which read that God **made us what we are**, connote a desire to make God responsible for some of the imperfections and vile inclinations to which modern man has succumbed.

We are God's workmanship and God created our bodily temples. We are responsible to love our bodies, to nurture them, and to care for them. God has given us our own free wills, that we may love, cherish and nurture our bodies, or, alternately abuse them and waste them as some are inclined to do.

God is not responsible for the evil way some misuse their bodies.

Ephesians 5:33

AV	...and the wife see that she **reverence** her husband.
D-R	...and let the wife **fear** her husband.
KJ21	...and the wife see that she **reverence** her husband.
TMB	...and the wife see that she **reverence** her husband.

CEV	...each wife should **respect** her husband.
GW	...and wives should **respect** their husbands.
NAB	...and the wife should **respect** her husband.
NASBU	...and the wife must see to it that she **respects** her husband.
NIV	...and the wife must **respect** her husband.
NJB	...and let every wife **respect** her husband.
NKJ	...and let the wife see that she **respects** her husband.
NLT	...and the wife must **respect** her husband.
NRSV	...and a wife should **respect** her husband.
OxI	...and a wife should **respect** her husband.
REB	...and the wife must show **reverence** for her husband.
TEV	...every wife must **respect** her husband.

Comment

The various choices of words here represent a fundamental difference between the historic biblical view of spousal relationships and the contemporary view. **Reverence** connotes a relationship which is sacred and sanctified by God. It is a much more powerful and meaningful word than the word **respect**. But in contemporary society, the reverencing of a husband by a wife is considered demeaning to the dignity of the wife. This latter point of view pits spousal *rights* against each other and is foreign to the historic Jewish-Christian concept of marriage being a relationship of mutual servanthood. It tends to reduce the institution of marriage from a sacred relationship to a secular, civil arrangement, to be established, regulated, or set aside by government fiat. This use of the word **reverence** in Traditional Bibles (and some contemporary modern versions) is therefore of singular importance to the attainment of a godly domestic relationship.

1 Timothy 1:5

AV	Now the end of the **commandment is charity**...
D-R	Now the end of the **commandment is charity**...
KJ21	Now the aim of the **commandment is charity**...
TMB	Now the aim of the **commandment is charity**...

CEV	You must **teach people to have genuine love**...
GW	My goal in giving you this **order is for love to flow from a pure heart**...
NAB	The aim of **this instruction is love**...
NASBU	But the goal of our **instruction is love**...
NIV	The goal of this **command is love**...
NJB	The final goal at which this **instruction aims is love**...
NKJ	Now the purpose of the **commandment is love**...
NLT	The purpose of my **instruction** is that all the Christians there would be filled with **love that comes from a pure heart**...
NRSV	But the aim of such **instruction is love** that comes from a pure heart...
OxI	But the aim of such **instruction is love**...
REB	This **instruction has love as its goal**...
TEV	The purpose of this **order is to arouse the love** that comes from a pure heart...

Comment

Traditional Bibles use the word **love** many times, but in certain places **love** is inadequate. This example is one of them, and further illustrates the higher level of linguistic and theological refinement of Traditional Bibles by comparison with contemporary versions. The latter lose the important distinction between **charity** and **love**.

See also 1 Corinthians 13:13 where St. Paul states that however important faith, hope and charity are, the greatest of these is **charity**.

1 Timothy 1:10b

AV	...for them that defile themselves with mankind...
D-R	...for them who defile themselves with mankind...
KJ21	...for those who defile themselves with mankind...
TMB	...for those who defile themselves with mankind...

CEV	...or who live as homosexuals...
GW	...homosexuals...
NAB	...sodomites...
NASBU	...and homosexuals...
NIV	...perverts...
NJB	...homosexuals...
NKJ	...sodomites...
NLT	...for homosexuals...
NRSV	...sodomites...
OxI	...male prostitutes...
REB	...perverts...
TEV	...sexual perverts...

Comment

Contrast the relative level of elegance of the Traditional Bibles with the mundane language of Contemporary Bibles in discussing a reprehensible practice.

Also note a powerful value judgment inherent in the use of the word **defile**, found in Traditional Bibles only, when applied to **homosexuals**. The traditional texts reflect a value judgment which, in our times, needs to be most boldly and specifically emphasized.

Titus 2:9

AV	Exhort **servants** to be obedient unto their own masters...
D-R	Exhort **servants** to be obedient to their masters...
KJ21	Exhort **servants** to be obedient unto their own masters...
TMB	Exhort **servants** to be obedient unto their own masters...

CEV	Tell **slaves** always to please their owners by obeying them...
GW	Tell **slaves** who are believers...
NAB	**Slaves** are to be under the control of their masters...
NASBU	Urge **bondslaves** to be subject to their own masters...
NIV	Teach **slaves** to be subject to their masters in everything...
NJB	**Slaves** must be obedient to their masters in everything...
NKJ	Exhort **servants** to be obedient to their own masters...
NLT	**Slaves** must obey their masters...
NRSV	Tell **slaves** to be submissive to their masters...
OxI	Tell those who are **enslaved**...
REB	**Slaves** are to respect their masters' authority...
TEV	**Slaves** are to submit themselves to their masters...

Comment

Practically all Contemporary Bibles use the word **slaves** in place of **servants**, whereas the Traditional Bibles and several conservative versions use **servants**. Why the difference?

Marxists and their modern counterparts have always advocated that servants (workers) be defiant to their masters (employers), advocating that they "rise up and throw off their chains." Hence the godly biblical admonition in Titus 2:9, and in numerous citations elsewhere in the Bible, that servants should be obedient to their masters, becomes for them intolerable. Most modern translators desire to limit the application of this godly admonition of obedience to as few people as possible; they change the word **servants** to **slaves,** thereby limiting its application to a tiny fragment of contemporary society. See also Romans 6:16, Romans 6:22, and many other biblical passages where the word **servant** has been changed to **slaves** in Contemporary Bibles.

In the Old and New Testaments of the *Authorized Version* the word **slave**(slaves) is used only twice; in the NIV, 160 times; in the NRSV, 293 times. These differences reflect differences in social agenda.

Hebrews 12:9

AV   ...we have had fathers of our flesh which corrected us, and we gave them **reverence**...

D-R   Moreover we have had fathers of our flesh, for instructors, and we **reverenced** them...

KJ21   ...we have had fathers of our flesh who corrected us, and we gave them **reverence**.

TMB   ...we have had fathers of our flesh who corrected us, and we gave them **reverence**.

CEV   ...and we still **respect** them.

GW   ...and we **respect** them.

NAB   ...and we **respected** them.

NASBU   ...and we **respected** them...

NIV   ...and we **respected** them for it.

NJB   ...and we **respected** them for it...

NKJ   ...and we paid them **respect**.

NLT   Since we **respect** our earthly fathers...

NRSV   ...and we **respected** them.

OxI   ...and we **respected** them.

REB   Again, we paid **due respect**...

TEV   ...and we **respected** them.

Comment

Contrast the basic principle of **reverence** toward earthly fathers in Traditional Bibles with the less powerful word **respect** in all Contemporary Bibles. Again, in the Traditional Bibles, the powerful word **reverence** is applied to a spiritually rich relationship between fathers and children, another relational concept which has been denigrated in current secular society. For almost two thousand years of Christian history, and prior to the advent of the gender-neutral agenda, this godly advice has been applied broadly and routinely to both fathers and mothers. It is only in the last half of the twentieth century that the beautiful word **reverence** in reference to family relationships has, for political reasons, been demeaned.

1 John 5:7

AV   For there are three that bear record in heaven,
the **Father**, the **Word**, and the **holy Ghost**: and
these three are one.

D-R   And there are three who give testimony in heaven, the
Father, the **Word**, and the **Holy Ghost**. And these three
are one.

KJ21 For there are three that bear record in Heaven:
the **Father**, the **Word**, and the **Holy Spirit;** and
these three are one.

TMB   For there are three that bear record in Heaven: the
Father, the **Word**, and the **holy Ghost**: and these three
are one.

CEV	(omitted)
GW	(omitted)
NAB	(omitted)
NASBU	(omitted)
NIV	(omitted)
NJB	(omitted)
NKJ	For there are three who bear witness in heaven: the **Father**, the **Word**, and the **Holy Spirit**...
NLT	(omitted)
NRSV	(omitted)
OxI	(omitted)
REB	(omitted)
TEV	(omitted)

Comment

In Traditional Bibles, the Trinity, namely, the **Father**, the **Son** (Word), and the **Holy Ghost** are specifically mentioned. They are omitted here in most Contemporary Bibles. Could not this recent exclusion from English translations reflect a subtle effort by secularist and unbelieving socio-linguists to subvert the whole orthodox concept of the Trinitarian nature of God?

The compiler is well aware of the controversy over the so-called *Johannine comma*. But those persons who doubt the authenticity of traditional wording have never adequately explained why it has appeared in major Latin and English versions for over 1,400 years. For historic and traditional reasons these venerable and ancient words should be retained.

Revelation 10:6

AV   And sware by him...that there should be **time no longer.**
D-R   And he swore...That **time shall be no longer.**
KJ21   And he swore...that there should be **time no longer...**
TMB   And he swore...that there should be **time no longer...**

CEV   He made a promise... "You won't have to **wait any longer.**"
GW   He swore an oath... "There will be **no more delay.**"
NAB   ...and swore... "There shall be **no more delay.**"
NASBU   ...and swore by Him who lives forever and ever...that there will be **delay no longer.**
NIV   And he swore... "There will be **no more delay!**"
NJB   ...and swore by him who lives for ever and ever... **The time of waiting is over...**
NKJ   ...and swore...that there should be **delay no longer...**
NLT   And he swore... **"God will wait no longer."**
NRSV   ...and swore... "There will be **no more delay...**"
OxI   ...and swore... "There will be **no more delay...**"
REB   ...and swore... "There shall be **no more delay...**"
TEV   ...and took a vow... "There will be **no more delay!**"

Comment

Traditional Bibles allude to the timelessness of eternity and point to an eternal circumstance which totally transcends the temporal. Most Contemporary Bibles allude to the coming of judgment using an earthly time frame.

Traditional Bibles allude to the unutterable gulf which separates the realm *time* from the realm *eternity*. Contemporary Bibles speak of God's impatience with evil on earth.

Traditional Bibles imply that God does not have the impatience of mortals and may be taking His time in arranging for the eternity of a timeless Heaven.

Conclusion

We who prepared this study prayerfully hope that this little book will, to some degree, alert both the lay reader and the scholarly community alike to the dangers which current political and cultural biases in contemporary Bible translations pose to the very foundation of 3,000 years of Jewish-Christian culture. The secularist battle for the hearts and souls of men is being fought not only on the theological level, but also on the social, political, and linguistic level through the vehicle of contemporary alterations in the historic Word.

Hopefully, goodly and godly souls will be inspired to join us in our efforts to combat this spreading threat to truth and virtue. We welcome the help of believers from academia, the churches, and all segments of the public at large in exposing the moral and cultural errancy of many modern Bible translations. It is an urgent task. Our work has only begun.

We earnestly pray that others will join with us in a commitment to accurate and faithful proclamation of the eternal, divinely-inspired and preserved Word of God.